to Marie-Sophie from Flossy

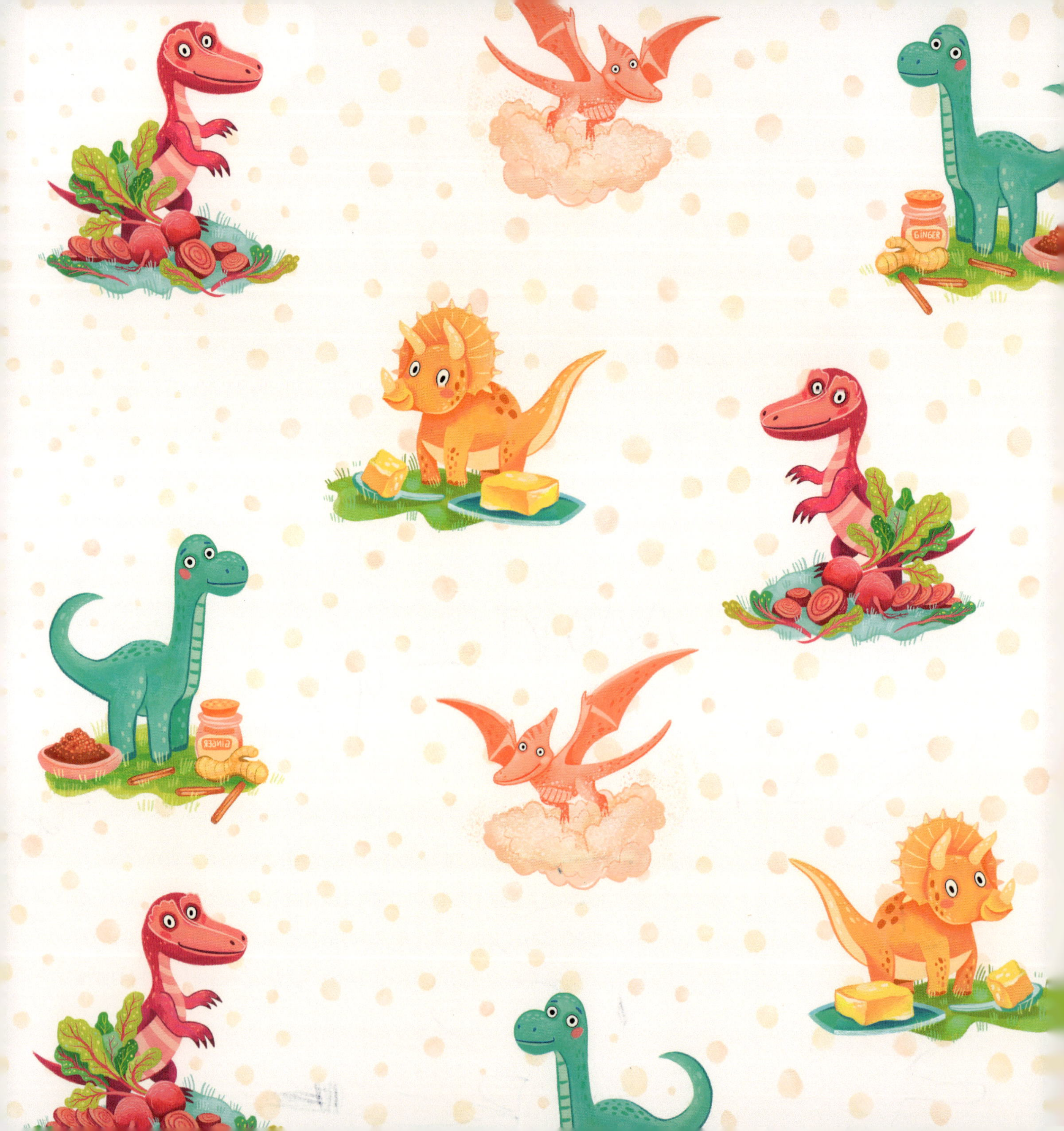
GINGER

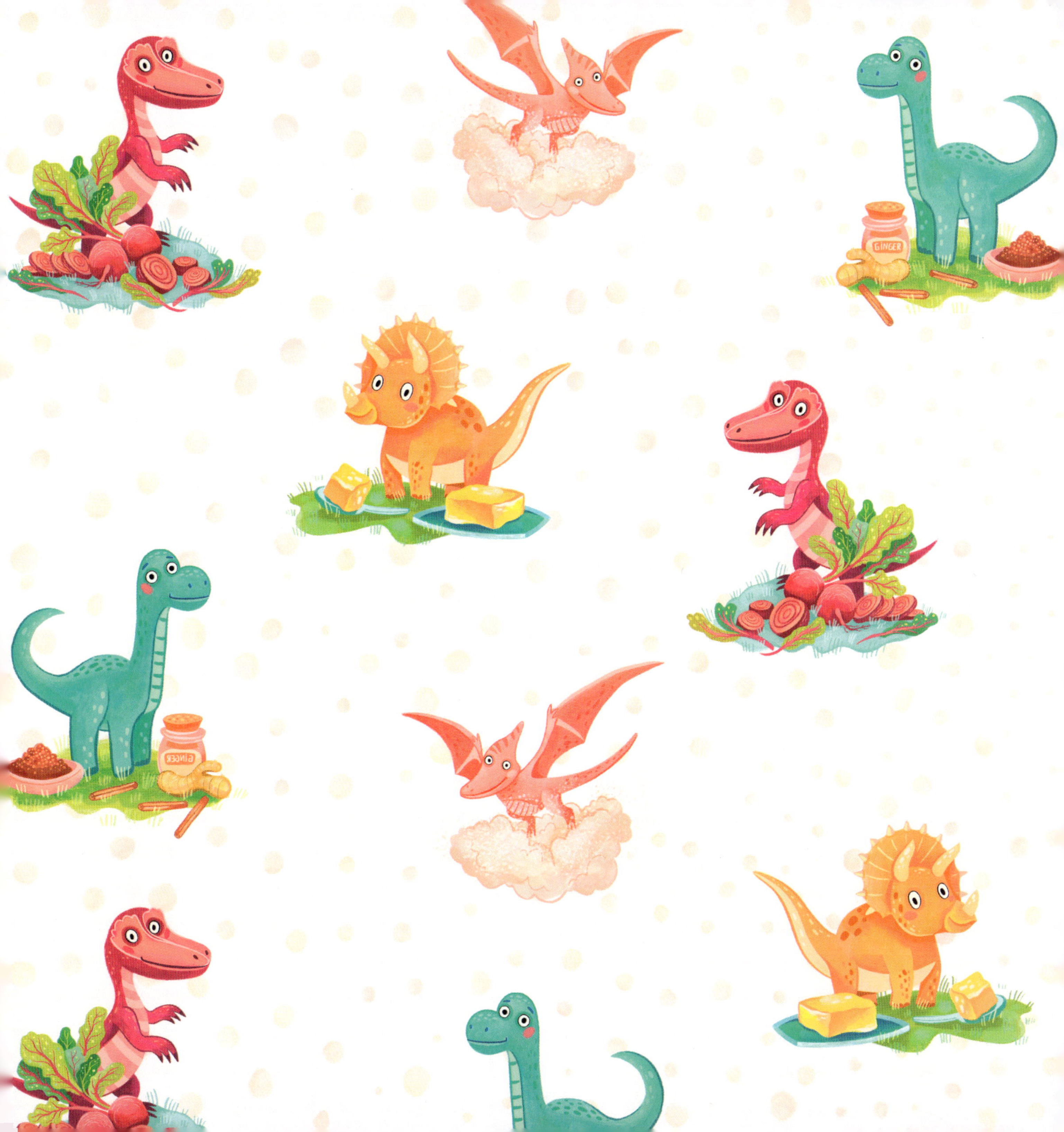
GINGER

"To all the parents who were brave enough to serve BEETROOT to their children."

# I will Never Ever eat Beetroot

written by
**ANA BALL**

illustrated by
**ANASTASIIA BIELIK**

# Grandma loves BEETROOT

*— it's on every shelf of her cupboard*

# Daddy loves BEETROOT
– it's in every corner of our garden

Mum loves BEETROOT — it's on every t-shirt she wears

And even our dog Pretsel loves BEETROOT
— it's all over his muzzle!

But Jimmy and I

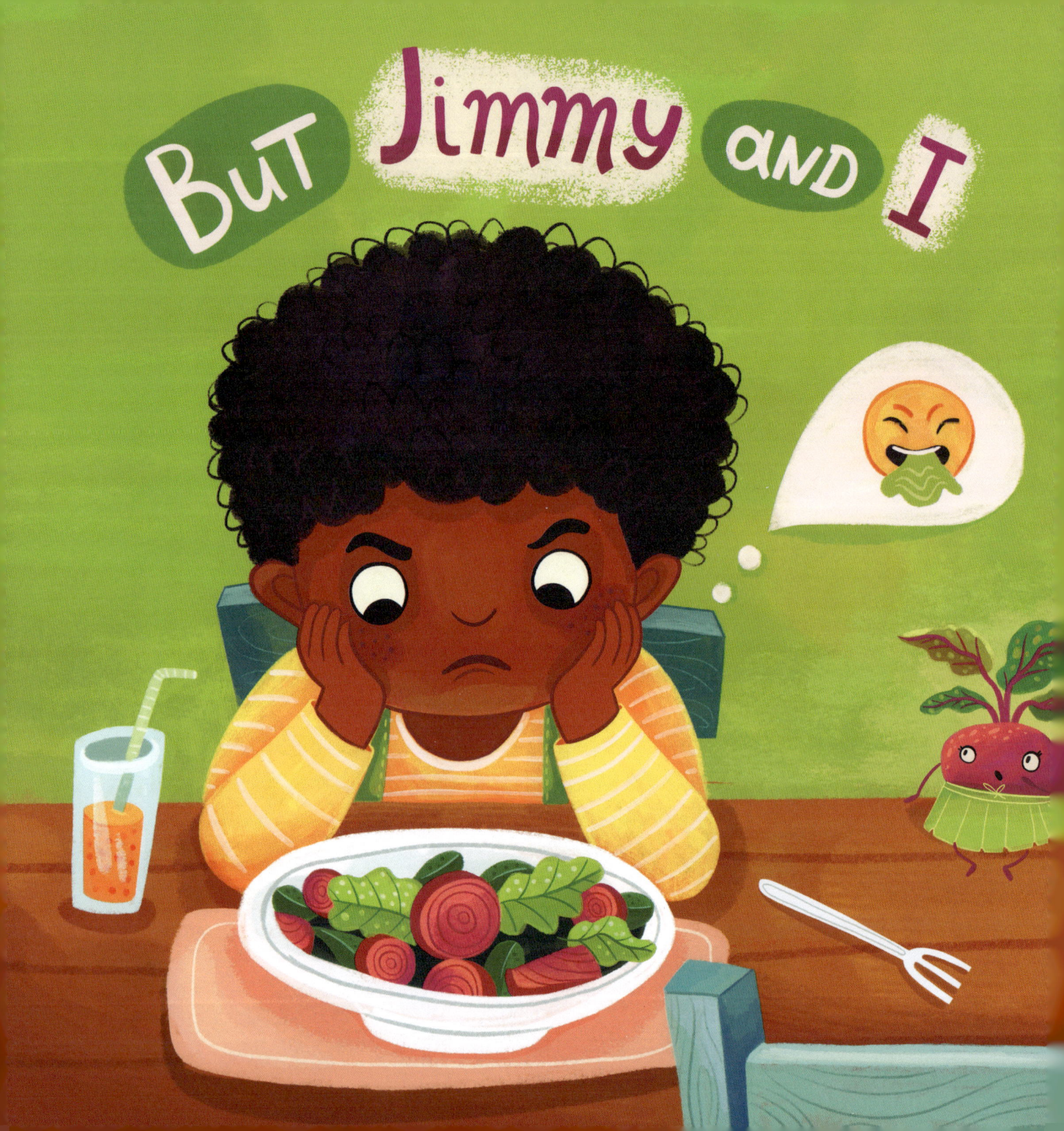

will NEVER EVER eat BEETROOT

IT'S TOO... PURPLE

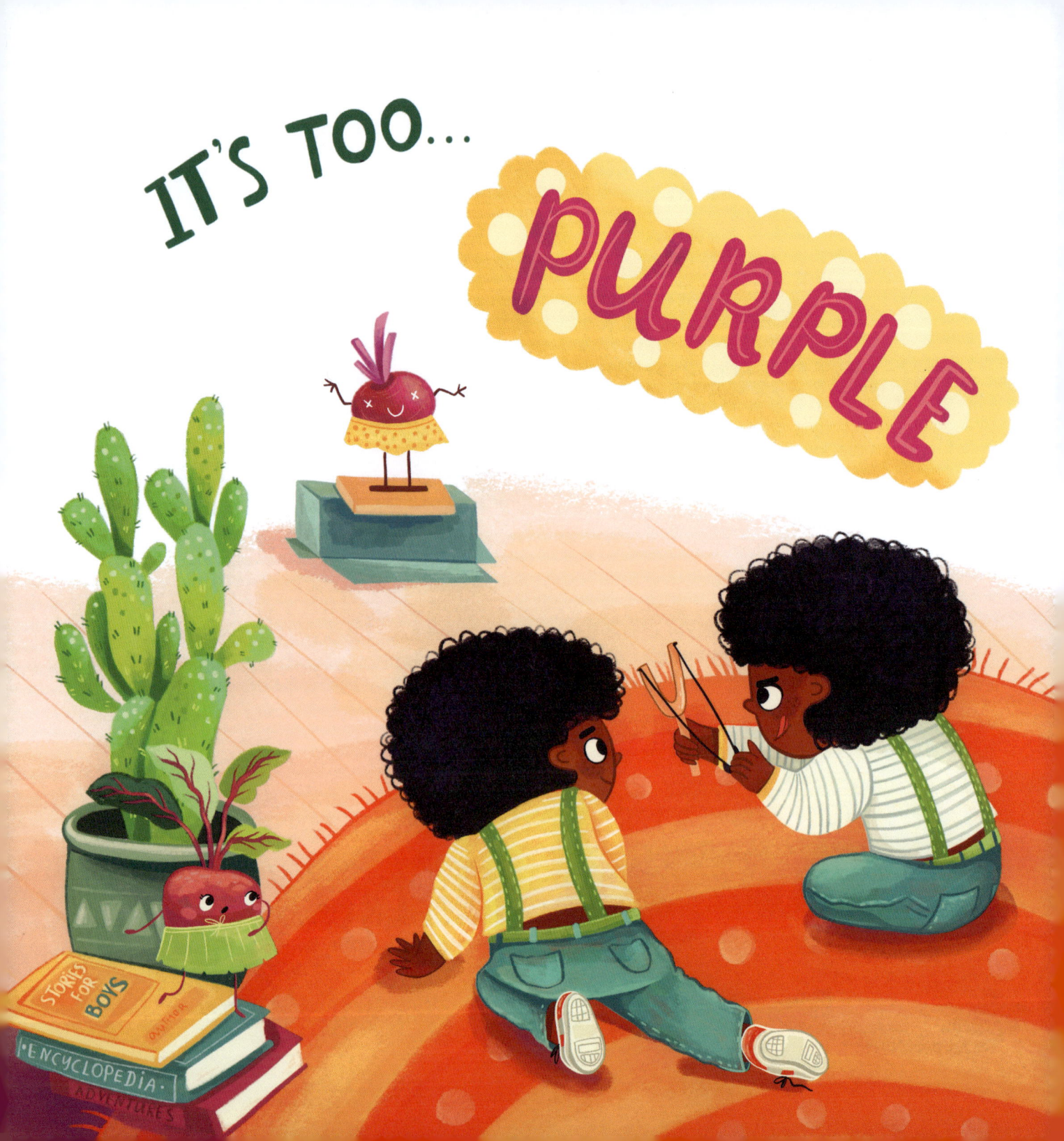

IT'S TOO... ROUND

It STAINS EVERYTHING it touches!

# It smells like NOTHING we have tried before!

# And it BEHAVES
## Like no other vegetable does!

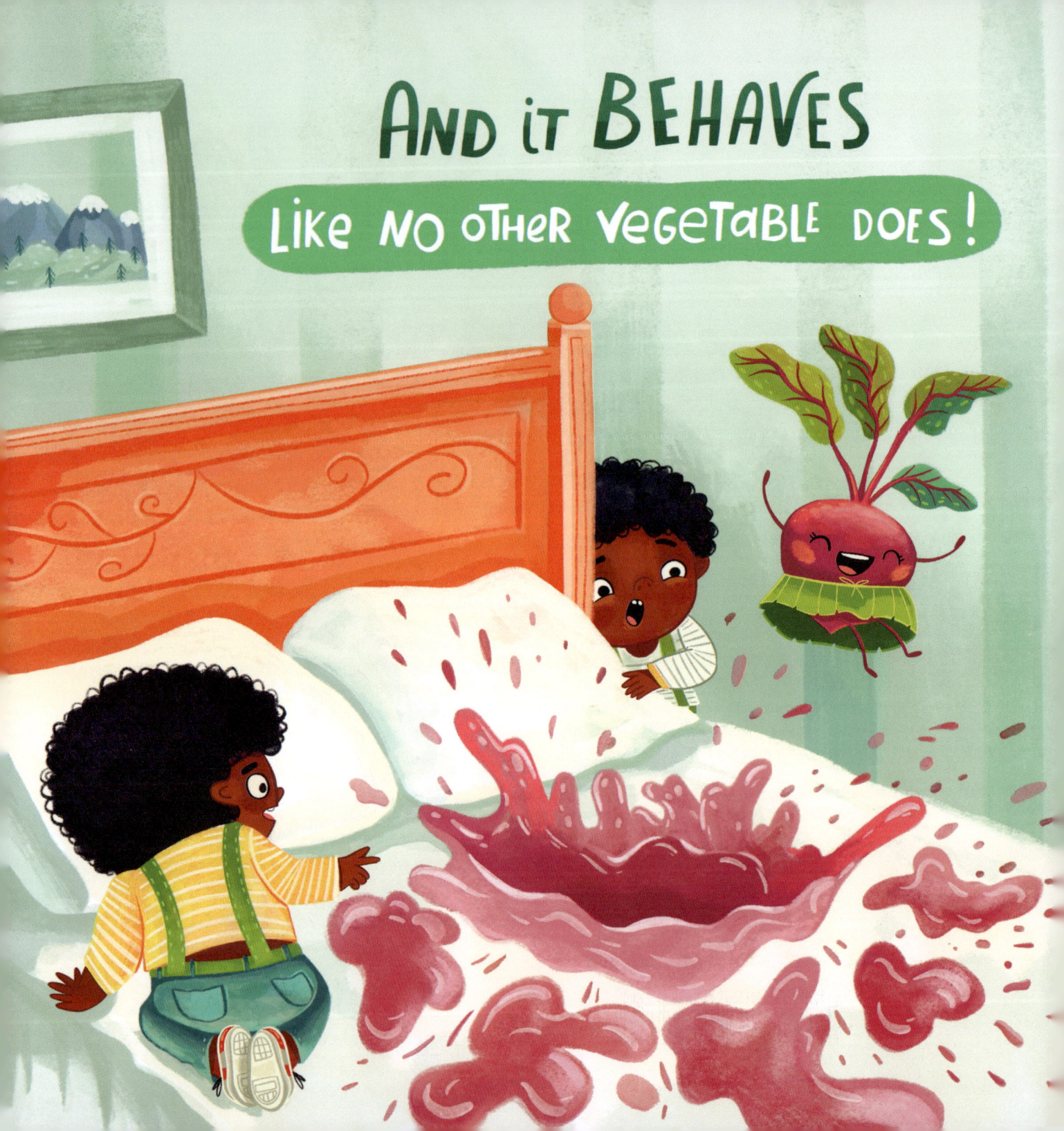

If there was a veggie JAIL,

BEETROOT WOULD DEFINITELY BE THERE!

My grandpa says he does not like BEETROOT either, but he can make yummy T-REX cookies if we set BEETROOT FREE...

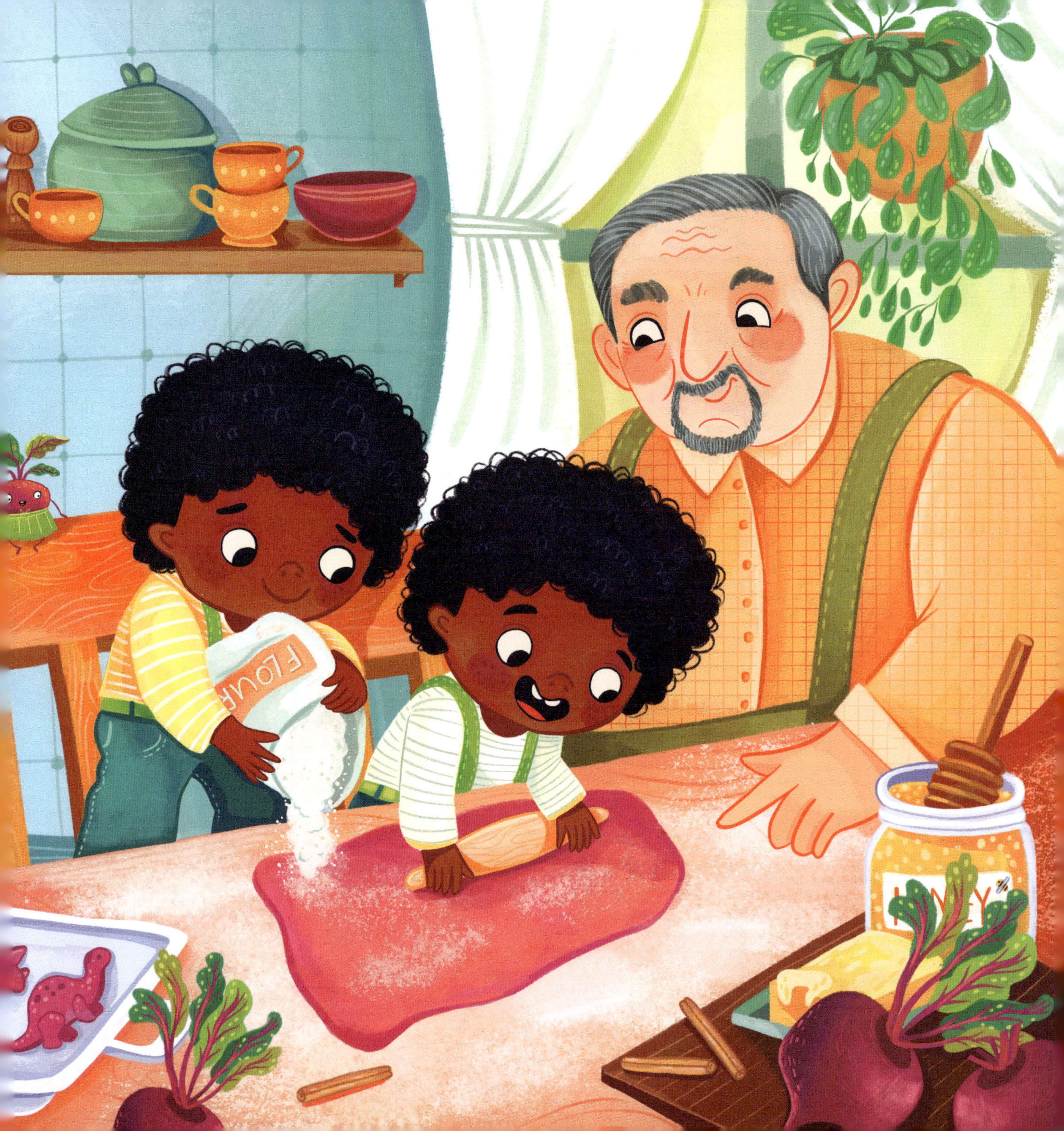
FLOUR

They are the **COLOUR** of a mighty **VELOCIRAPTOR**

They make you **STRONGER** than a **TRICERATOPS**

They make you **TALLER** than a **BRONTOSAURUS**

They make you **FLY** like a **PTERODACTYL**

AND they are SUPER-DUPER DELICIOUS!

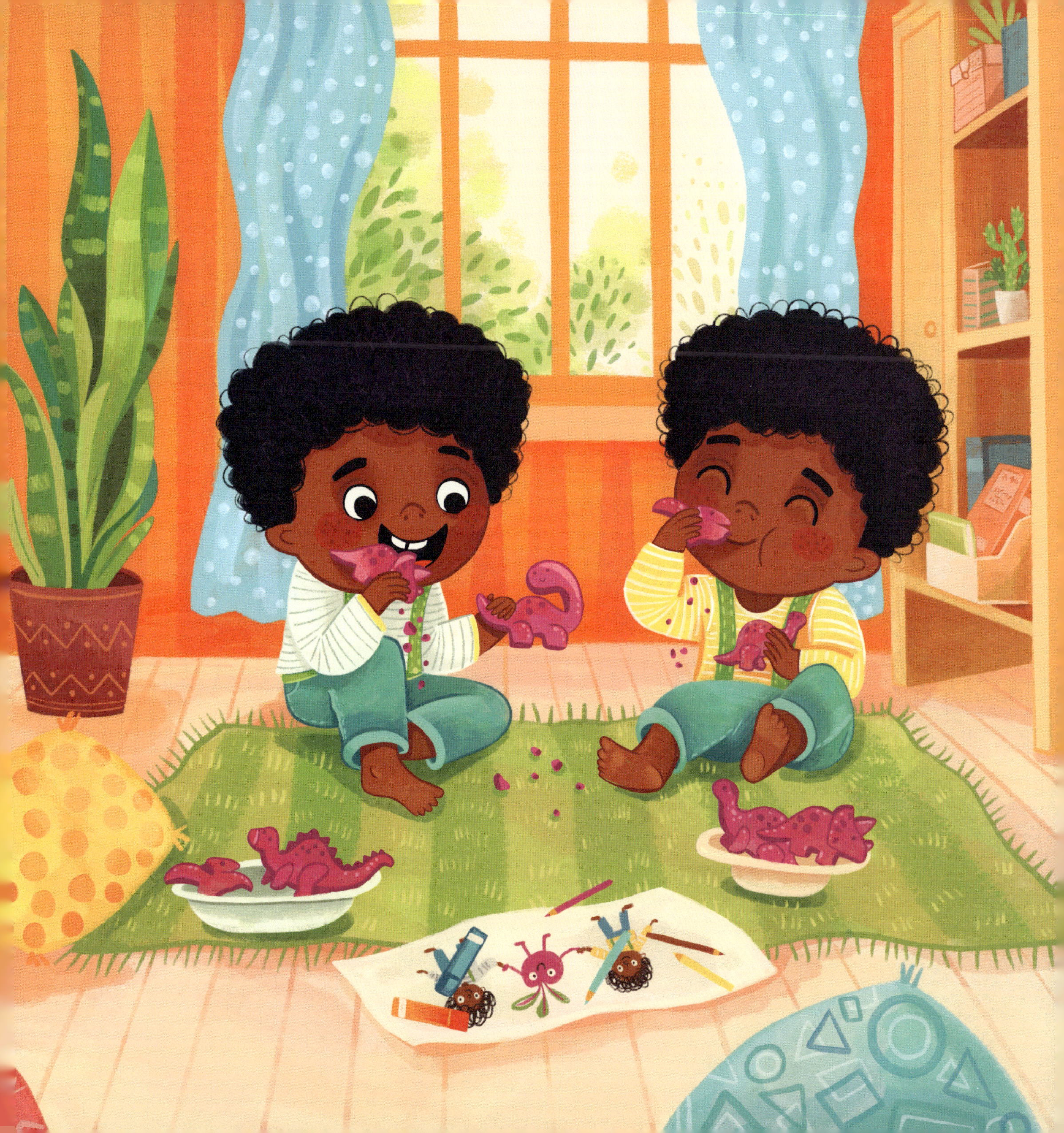

# T-REX COOKIES
(makes 20 cookies)

## INGREDIENTS
- 2 small beetroots (about 140g)
- 180g (about 1.5 cups) self-rising flour
- 45g butter, melted
- 5 tablespoons runny honey, divided
- 1 tablespoon ground cinnamon
- 1 tablespoon ground ginger

# METHOD

1. Preheat the oven to 180 C.
2. Boil or steam beetroot until soft (around 30 minutes).
3. Roughly chop your beetroot and mash it until it is smooth.
4. Combine mashed beetroot with melted butter and flour.
5. Add 4 tablespoons of honey, cinnamon and ginger and mix well to form the dough.
6. Roll out the dough and cut out shapes using cookie cutter.
7. Bake for 12-15 minutes until a wooden cocktail stick comes out clean.
8. Lightly glaze with honey (optional).
9. Enjoy!

# My Lava smoothie

### (feeds 2 small tummies)

**1 cup milk** (dairy or dairy free alternative)

**1/2 cup frozen berries** (raspberries or blueberries work best)

**2/3 cup of frozen pineapple**

**1/2 small raw beetroot, roughly chopped**

### METHOD:

1. Add all the ingredients into a food processor and blend for 1-2 minutes until smooth.
2. Pour into 2 cups.
3. Add straws.
4. **ENJOY!**

# Volcano Pasta

*feeds 4 small tummies*

## Optional Toppings
- feta cheese
- Roasted sunflower seeds
- Roasted pine nuts

**Ingredients:**
- 4 cloves of garlic, finely chopped
- 200 g spaghetti
- 100 g Greek yogurt
- 1 big beetroot, cooked or raw
- 1/2 onion, finely chopped
- 100 ml pasta water

## Method:
1. Add pasta to boiling water and cook according to instruction on a package.
2. While pasta is cooking, fry onion and garlic.
3. To make a beetroot sauce, combine peeled and chopped beetroot, garlik, onion, yogurt and pasta water in a food processor and mix well.
4. Transfer the beetroot sauce into a pan and mix with cooked pasta.
5. Add toppings to your taste.
6. Enjoy!

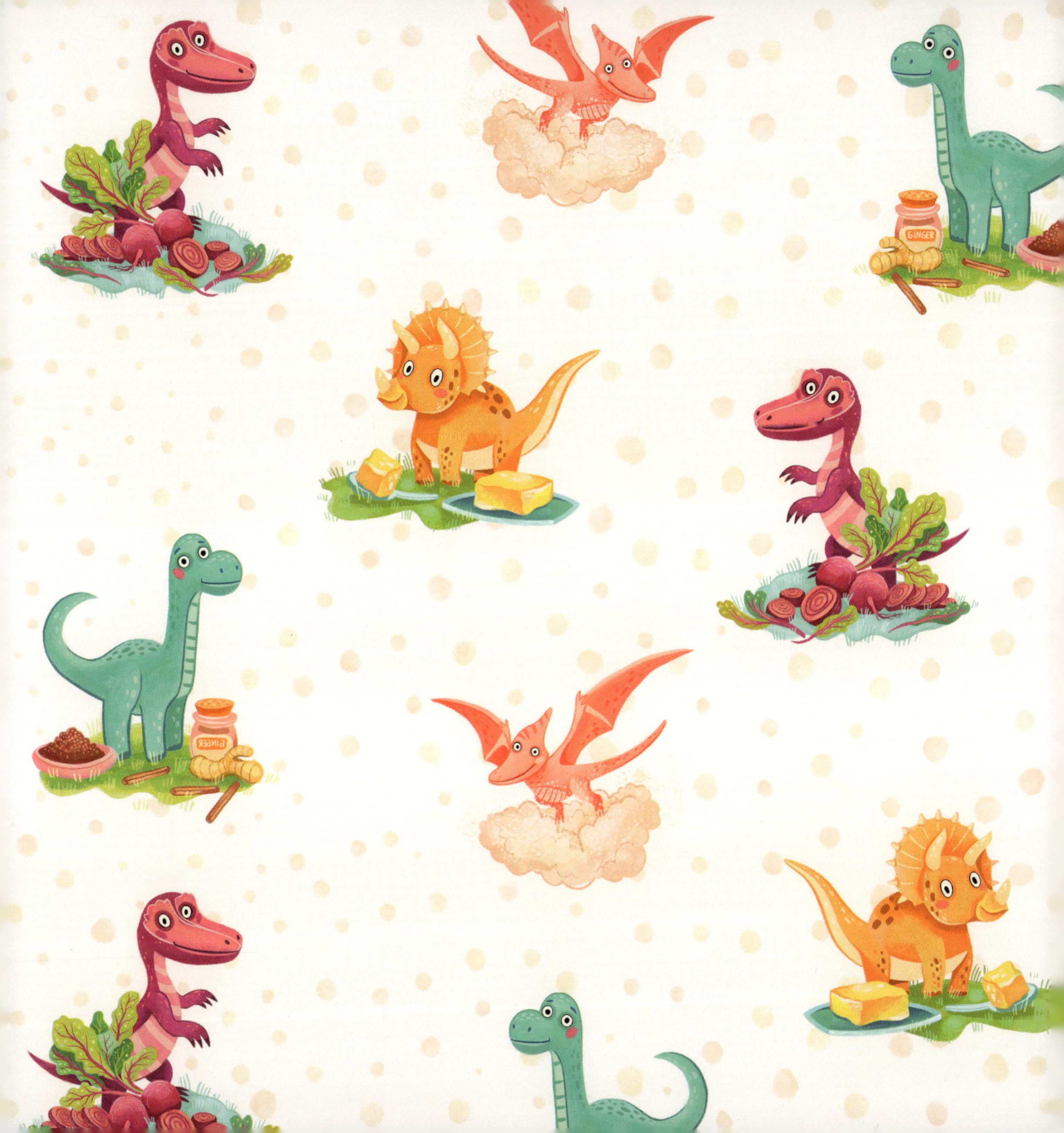
GINGER

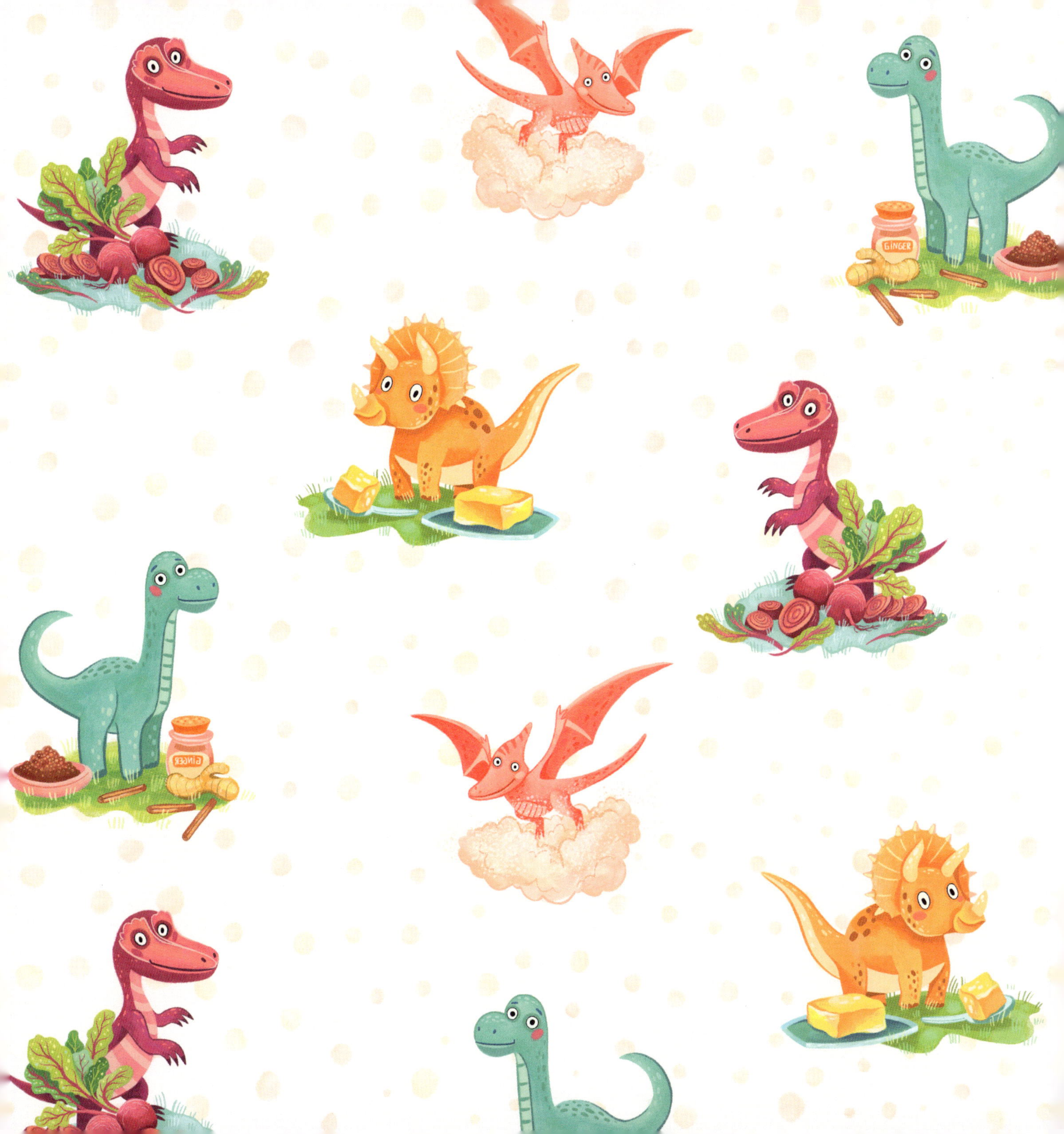
GINGER

Printed in Great Britain
by Amazon